Life
From Where I Stand

To: Bob Daughery

by
Louise Flynn Underhill

Louise Flynn Underhill

5/3/97

Jelm Mountain Press

1991

Life
From Where I Stand.
Then and Now.

Cover photo: Gerhard Studio, St. Louis, MO., 1945

Send orders to
1815 Russell Ave, Cheyenne, WY. 82001

Jelm Mountain Press
Laramie, Wyoming 82070
ISBN 0-936204-80-X pa.

Dedicated to friends of long ago who have gone ahead,
to friends and loved ones now,
and to those I've still to meet.

Authority!
No.
Observer?
Yes.
And if you think
I speak
with knowing voice,
believe me
I have seen it.

Contents

Then

Now

A LONG WAY

I've come a long way
from sliding down hay stacks
or playing in a bin of newly threshed wheat,
from walking down dark roads
with my hand held tight by Dad's
or sailing on imagined seas
about the sidewalk of our house;
or playing war with sticks for guns
and marching at school to orders
given by one whose brother fought.

I've come a long way
from dreams of going to Ireland
or France or seeing a play
in London's busy Palladium;
or enjoying the heart of Hawaii
or climbing Mexican peaks.
I've walked the streets of Nome
and wandered about downtown in New York,
a long, long way from home.

Today I sit and ponder
how one poor child alone
could do so much and see so much
and still just wish for more.
It's been a long long time
and I've come a long long way.

WOULD YOU BELIEVE?

That chubby child
I was so long ago
Was dressed in uniform
And from the teacher's desk
I sang of nurses on a battlefield.

I still can sing that song
Though more than four score
Busy years have passed.
My memory is strong.

And once again I am
The child who helped
In my own way
To sell the bonds
We used to pay
For World War I.

(Recently Cousin Minnie Pearl on Nashville Now stated this was
also her World War I experience.)

DREAM

MY MIND PLAYS OVER ANCIENT TIMES
WHEN I WAS HAPPY, SCARED OR SAD
AND MIXES THEM WITHOUT A PLAN
TO HAUNT MY SLEEP OR THRILL AGAIN
AND THIS I CALL A DREAM.

WISHES

I used to wish upon a star
a four-leafed clover too
a wishbone and a cardinal
and on an old horseshoe.
There were so many ways to wish
and few of them came true
I guess I was a dreamer then
but now there are so few
I'd like to go back to childhood
and start it all anew.

'TIS TRUE

You never know how much you have
until it's gone.
You never know where you are going
until you lose your way.
You never know how much you owe
to someone else
until that one has left
to find another love.
That is life!

JULESBURG FAMILY

I wondered as I went again
to visit that old home I'd loved,
what memories would haunt me there
for that had been a year I'd live
forever in my sweetest dreams.
There was the open door to take me in;
the family portraits on the shelves,
the table stretched out full and long
was once again piled high with food
and so, I felt at home.

Not Eric in the master's chair
nor on the porch to talk to friends;
no Esther, dimpling as she thought
of other foods she might have set
but Wilma in her blue chiffon
and Fred outside were holding forth;
Mildred bustled as her mother once had done
and wondered if she had enough for all
and Burl, as he always had,
sat and watched and listened,
while Vern and Myron visited
with friends of long ago,
short images of their father,
and Alvin, looking more like him than all
played host or held the babes.

And now here come a group of youth
all tall and strong and separate
yet bearing on their faces imprints
of a sturdy Swedish breed,
in their arms their offspring,
whole families of tender young
and babies dear,
loved and contented.

Yes, the old house haunts me,
not with ghosts of those long dead
but memories of days and nights
filled to the brim with life and love,
and those departed now who shared them then
look down on all our joy from up above
and are content.

"I LOVE YOU"

"I love you."
These three words
whispered in my ear
did something for my spirit
I cannot quite explain.
"I love you."
I live so far away
I sometimes lose the feel
of just belonging
but
"I love you"
brings again
that feel of worth.

LOST

That storm that threatened all the day had struck
and sheets of rain were pouring down upon the spot
where I had left my car. I turned to watch the flood,
just as my car rolled slowly into the street.
I pushed through dampened folk between me and
the door
when one quick hand slid out and grasped my purse.
I was aghast,
for suddenly I knew I had no proof of my identity.
My cards, my cash, my keys were there.
That slip that told me in what rooming house
I'd left my aged mother.
What could I do? My whole existence lay
within that purse and I was lost.
How could I find the thief? and true,
when I had found the one with clutching hand
what proof had I that purse was mine?
I turned my thoughts to her who trustingly
awaited my return. I shook with grief.
Suddenly I awoke.
Through the years long since
that nightmare has disturbed my dreams, my life.

OLD LADIES

I liked old Nan,
she was, indeed,
a bore sometimes
and so am I.

I liked old Ruth,
she was, it's truth
so proud of what she did,
and so am I.

I liked old Beth,
she never feared
to try what she could do.
no more have I.

I liked old Jane.
Her life of sin
left scars on soul and mind,
and so has mine.

MARIAN

Tender and tough he said of her
good hearted and sharp tongued I said
and in this age of ours she was unique,
for whom do you know of whom it could be said,
You always knew what she thought of you
long years before you heard
"she's dead."

AN IDOL

Miss Nancy Grey
died yesterday
and my teenage heart was broken.

I sought her out
with a smile and a shout,
she was so sweetly spoken.

She worked in our bank,
so gracious and frank,
and always a rose at her place.

I scarcely believe
the whole world she'd deceived,
and yet she died in disgrace.

SECOND WIFE

Today you called me by her name
and though you did not know,
my heart rejoiced to be so called
for you had loved her so.

I did not weep as some might do
that you had named me thus
for love like yours cannot be hid
and in it I will grow.

SARAH

"Sarah, you've pestered me all my life.
Now go away and let me die in peace."
and though her life had all been spent
with John and their three sons, she went
not weeping as she might have done
had her soul been more sensitive,
but equal as she knew herself to be
and gentle though he was
she had heard him strike out before
but he had never touched to hurt
nor would he now.
Their years, not smooth
had all been hers
and when he went
she would be all alone,
a mastless ship.

AMY

My time is limited
I do not know that I will wake
Tomorrow.
And so I live today.
This room my haven;
I read, I sleep, I watch the sky.
My trees, my flowers, my birds,
Live by me and fill up my time
For I am part of all
The universe.

MISS JANE

Her house was small and snug and clean
and she was prissy too,
and when I heard she had a man
I hardly believed it true.
And then I watched both night and day,
she seemed discreet to me,
and how they ever found a way
I really could not see.
For theirs were times Victorian
their love they did not show
he came and went so quietly
there was no way to know
she was just his lady-love,
and not his family.

BUM

"A bum
that's what you are."
and from that love
my only scar
is that you died
before you knew
I thought you were
"a GOOD bum too."

SCATTERBRAIN

A scatterbrain they called me then
when I was very young,
a dreamer was the name I got
before I was twenty-one.
Why don't you watch your business
they asked throughout my years,
but since I've reached this golden age
the things I don't remember now
are just because I'm old.

THE SCOLD

She scolded here, she scolded there,
She scolded people everywhere
At her club, her church, her school,
She called each one she met a fool
And when she died, alone, this week
I wondered what in Heaven she'd seek
When I get to Heaven, I swear,
She'll be scolding Angels there.

MY MOM

How did she do the things she did
when we were growing up?
I know we questioned many times
why there was no more cash
and yet she managed food and clothes
and movies once a week.
How did she know when she could have
those ugly shoes she hated so
or one new dress she wanted then.
We could not always have the things
we thought we needed most,
but music lessons, books and school
were somehow on her list.
I've thought so many times since then
I'll never be the kind she was
but how I wish I had just once
told her so.

GRANDMOTHER

What charm did our grandmother have?
She told a story well,
I can recall from early youth.
She cooked up beans, cornbread and poke
and flavored them with pork and onion too.
She made up games for us to play
when first she baby-sat us three
and told us tales of long ago.
We knew she loved us, it was true
for she found things for us to do.

MIZ ALICE

Miz Alice lived not far from us
in genteel poverty and yet
there was no hint of this from her.
Her home was old and shared with those
who were her family.
Its greyish splendor hid the glow
of furniture, antique and fine,
the rosewood chairs her mother had:
the walls now lined with volumes rare.
In summer underneath the trees
she often sat to read and talk
and would ignore the mundane world
that swept along the busy street
of that main thoroughfare.
What has become of that type home
and that Victorian family?
I do not find them here or now
and yet they lent gentility
to all of us somehow.

HYPOCRITE

You taught me how to beg
and then you taught me true
how beggars could be treated
by hypocrites like you!

HIS TALL TALE

Of all the tales my husband told
I loved this one the best:
"I do not know where I belong,
I was not born on land," he said,
"My mother who was Dutch had gone
to see her family overseas
when on return to this, our land,
I was born before my time.
We were aboard an English ship
in waters called Canadian,
and so I have no native land
or else I can claim three."

It was a thrilling tale he told
and I would listen and agree.
He nowhere did belong
except to me.

CHARLES

Why do you thumb your nose at me,
and tip your hat just so,
for always I see you thus
as you do come and go.

Those gestures small were ones I loved
you made them with such daring
and as I think of them today,
by golly, you were caring.

THE ROYAL LOVE STORY

The Duchess of Windsor died today
an elderly lady of history,
the famous romance of my time
tinctured with pity and mystery.
Full fifty years ago
King Edward VIII gave up his throne
and ever through his years
they wandered about, alone,
for he was forbidden to make her his Queen
and gave up his crown for his wife.
It was a story often told
in tales that were read by girls long ago.

But just to know such things appear today
makes life worth while.

JOHN'S SONG

I opened my eyes this morning
I looked all around
I saw no candles burning
I heard no sacred sound
I couldn't smell the roses
I still was in my bed,
so this is what I thought:

"I guess I'll live instead."

SMILES

Her smile so firmly fixed
seems key to life for her;
where did she get that mirth
which bubbles up inside?
It was not bred from those
whose ancestry she bore
for other siblings were not so,
one sulked, one fought but none
was always happy as she was.
So we must understand
it was not heritage
it must have been some misplaced chromosome
within her heart and soul
that kept her smile intact
from birth throughout that long
and smiling life she lived.

DATED

Some books are dated.
Some people are too.
And as I watch a modern dance
I find I am. Are you?

WHO AM I?

Nicknames I knew
were tender, sweet
or mocking,
but even these
were not enough
to help me find
myself.

I ran away
I fell in love,
but even these
were not enough
to help me find
myself.

I lived my life
and put in verse
my inmost thoughts
and only now
do I begin
to know the one
I was,
and am not now.

CARESS

I LOVED EACH SWEET CARESS
ABOUT THEM I WOULD RAVE
EXCEPT YOU ALWAYS HOLD ME CLOSE
BEFORE YOUR MORNING SHAVE.

STOLEN LOVE

The hours fled
before we knew.
That time had come again,
our passions spent,
when we must rise and part.
I could not let you go.
You felt that way too
for afterwards you said,
when you had turned and left me,
"I had the greatest urge
to chase your taxi down the street."
And I — why — I called to you.
I dared not say a word.

THE OTHER WOMAN'S LOSS

When they said
you were dead,
I could not grieve
for through the years
I hid my fears
that you would leave.

I could not weep
as widows do
for I had always shared
another's love for you.
She wept; I grieved
and turned a smiling face
for all the world to see.

YOUR GODS

Only money?
Or pleasure?
Leisure?
Romance?
Fun?
All these
supplant
the great God of our fathers,
WORK.

DISILLUSIONMENT

But yesterday she spoke with awe
of him who now she can only hate.
The courting was so wonderful
reality could wait.
As lover he was most supreme:
as husband he was not a mate.

JUDAS

What strange emotion led
a traitor to the fold of Christ?
How had he found his way
into that inner group?
And having walked that way,
what hoped this man to gain
who sold his Lord for thirty coins?
What strange emotion filled the breast
of Judas, the betrayer?

AUNT LIL'S DEVOTIONALS

She took us up to the mountain top
and urged that we live up there,
but her mountains were grassy Missouri hills
not Rocky Mountains high and bare.
You cannot live on the highland peaks
surrounded by ice and snow,
where ever come the storms about,
with the ease of those below,
and so I returned
to my lowland home
surrounded by people and fears,
but do you know I've remembered
her talks through all these years.

LENGTH OF LIFE

In eighteen hundred nine
two famous men were born.
In eighteen forty nine
the best known then was dead.
The other was a failure and unknown
outside his native state.

Who were these men?
The first was Edgar Allen Poe,
the other was Abe Lincoln.
And what this record says to me:
No one ever knows, each has his time.

For some the years are few
while others wait till they are old
to make their mark.
To each one there's a time
when he completes the task
for which he came to earth
and when he has he leaves.

That boy at fifteen who had reached his peak
and then at eighteen left this earth
had made his mark as surely
as one who little knew his skills
till he had reached full half a century.

Each one fulfilled his destiny
and then moved on.

CHRISTIANS

We Christians are a curious lot
who strangely play our role.
There are the ones who scarcely know
they have a newborn soul.

Then there are the others
who go through life like a mole
and being straight and narrow
can walk through a key hole.

We Christians are a curious lot
each turned that way or this
and, oh, how much of God's own grace
so many of us miss.

PLEA BARGAIN

Can I plea bargain, Lord,
when I stand at the throne
on Judgement Day? I will again
be pleading what I did to offset
those great goods I might have done.
Can I plea bargain, Lord?

Can I plea bargain, Lord?
If I plead guilty to neglect,
can I get off those other sins
that were so wrong?
Can I plea bargain then
or just be glad that I have been
pardoned all those other errors
by my faith in thee?

JOBS

"If you should meet your Master today
and He said, 'I have a job for you.'
What would you say?"
Moses said, "Oh, I can't do that
for I can't speak well."
Jonah said, "Why should I go there?"
and went the other way.
And Sarah, from her hiding place,
just heard Him say to Abraham
"You shall be father of mankind."
And what did she say —
she laughed so loud He heard her
and she said, "How can I? I'm too old,
and so is he." But they did.

WHO?

Master of Destiny,
who can that be?
Teacher or writer,
policeman or me.

HATE

"Father, forgive," I breathed
and slept again secure.
So happy that the depths I saw
within myself were just a dream.
That deep emotion bared
I did not know I had
for never in my years —
a full lifetime for man —
had I come face to face
with so much hidden hate
within myself.
Thank God, I had within me too
an understanding of forgiveness
bringing peace.

READING GUIDES OUR LIVES

I could but see from where I sat
acres and acres of earth so flat.
I heard a voice say mountain land
and wondered if I had to stand
To see the peaks that one could see,
they certainly were too far from me.
There was a child in days of yore
who read much of mountain lore
and many books about the sea.
That child was me.

SAPPHO

Three men I gave to history;
Him whose photographs gave my words life:
Him whose drawings brought one book to be:
And him I loved whose name I bear
That is entombed this century as mine.

.

LIVING ON THE EDGE

I live so often on the edge of happenings;
while others climb, I watch;
while others dance, I sing;
and so one night my brashness
that led to my quick quips
and brought a loving cup of brew
for all of us to share
amazed me.
For quick of wit
I laughed and shared
the center of attention
just this once.

THE CATACOMBS

I could not bring myself to go
down there within the Catacombs:
that inearthed city of the dead
whose narrow lanes wound endlessly
through corridor and hall
and back again
It was a cemetery
beneath the ground, and though
I came to see it on this trip
I sat in horror in the anteroom
and wept.

MEMORIES DO THIS TO US

"Four ducks on a pond,"
I never pass that ranch
without recalling the rhyme,
for there beside the road
upon that little pond,
the scene is laid before me:
Three tall trees are company there
and on the waters down below
the ducks in whiteness gleam,
while I in loneliness say,
"What a little thing to remember in tears,"
and go on my way.

WHAT IS A CHILD?

That child you held but now
within your eager arms
provides a kind of life
eternal, which the man
who has no child can never know.
He is your immortality
another generation of your self
to keep you ever in this world.

But he who has no son,
what can he do to secure
a place for his family name?

If he be builder, he can build;
If he be poet, he can write;
If he be artist, he can paint;
If he be teacher he can best
excite another mind
and so project himself into eternity.
But if his skills are few
he can but hope to have a child
to carry on his name
and so project himself
into the ages.

FRAGILE EARTH

Earth keeps reminding us of its
fragility...
a flood, a fire, a storm, a hurricane,
earthquake, tornado at its worst
are warnings that earth is not
eternal.

PREDICTION

The moon was once a blazing star
Today we know that Mars was too
And then we learn that here on earth
We have a core of lava in our heart
Will we, too, one day be a star
Or stone with nothing left but ash
To show our art, our skyscrapers, our wealth?

THE HUBBLE TELESCOPE

The Hubble telescope is not
man's first attempt to probe the skies
and it will not be last,
for when God plans for us to know
the story of the universe
we will succeed.

AROUND SATURN

Today
my mind is freed
from mundane matters here
for I am on
a planet
passing
trip.

ECLIPSE

When man in this all-knowing age
feels threatened by a sudden storm
and then recalls the tales
the ancient ones ascribed to it,
one can but wonder if with all
our vaunted learning we have come
away from superstition's edge
to what?

INSPIRATION

We must believe beyond what we can see
or there can be no poetry or song.
We must see angels where no man has been
and hear their glorious music once again.
For man without a dream or song or sight
is just a man, but given dreams or hopes
becomes a poet, singer for eternity.

FATE

Who is the one who fails
when that ill-fated jet goes down?
He doesn't make the flight
or yields his place to one
more eager to get on,
and yet you say there is no Power
that rules our lives.
I beg to differ
else you would be alive
and I be dead.

THE DERBY WINNER

For fifty years she tried
to find a colt to race
one time the famous course
at Churchill Downs, and win.
And now at ninety-two
she sat, a hatted dowager
who could have seen the race
more clearly on TV at home;
who could not hear the calls
until her manager
screamed them for her,
but when she knew she'd won
her look of unbelief, then joy
was wondrous to behold.
She won the Derby this very first time
she ever sent a colt to try.

Just what inspiration she gave me!

THE SCULPTRESS' HANDS

Her hands enchanted me
for they were warm and worn,
gnarled, but so expressive.
They formed the clay
upon the wheel and made a pot
or pinched off little bits of clay
and placed them here and there
to form a statue, or a taper tall.
They knew their task and did it.

WHAT IS PRAYER?

What is prayer, please?
A silent thanks for morning light,
A cry for help in threat or pain,
A plea for care for one we love,
A search for guidance or for truth,
All these and more, for prayer
is importuning God most ceaselessly
in hope, in love, in faith,
until we can accept His will.

FIRST CHRISTMAS

There's a song in the air
and a dream in the heart.
There's a babe in the straw
and a star in the sky.
There's a prophecy filled
on that first Christmas night
with a song in the air
and a dream in the heart.

CHRISTMAS CAROLING

It was still dark on Christmas morn,
we teens had gathered at the church
to go a-caroling at dawn.
The ground was white, the winter cold,
we muffled up our frosty ears
and laughed at steam our warm breath made
then through the snow we dashed.

The house was dark, we raised our song
of "peace on earth, good will to men,"
and when the lights went on, the curtain rose.
They stood there, the bearded man
and at his side, wrapped in her shawl
Aunt Maggie, as we knew her then
sang with us on the other side.

What memory that is of days long gone
but I who now am old
can see them yet and thrill again
as from the other side
their voices join with ours.

QUESTIONS

Questions, questions, questions,
life is full of questions;
What shall I wear?
Where do I go?
How strange it is
we hardly realize, but
we've spent our lives
answering questions.
Who are we now?
Where have we been?
What shall we do?
Where do we go?

Why is it so?

AWE INSPIRING

That awe inspiring One
who guided us today
through winds that tore
a trailered house from moorings
and hurled it helter-skelter
across our way
or placed a cloud at sunset
to shield us from the evening glow
oh, yes, He is the one
who layered rock
in ribbons grey and copper too
or set lone pillars on the plains
to mystify our human minds
and leave us questioning.

PRESERVATION

My past has been blotted out.
Scarce six weeks was I
upon this earth
when our house
was blown down by tornado.
The farm where once we lived
is part strip mine today,
its yellow fields piled up in rows.
The high school where I taught
was razed for parking lot,
and even my old home
has nothing left of ours
except the front porch swing.

Almost half a century ago
I came to live out West.
My roots in this new place too are gone.
A tall state building stands
where once I lived.

I am proud that verse of mine
was put this year into the cornerstone.
For now my name is here in history.

ANTIQUES

There's no accounting for tastes.
What one person thinks is junk
another one exclaims in awe,
"This is just what I want,
the best I've seen."
And so they wander round about
and look at many things,
then turn away or buy at once
the treasure that they found.

OPPORTUNITY'S WINDOW

Opportunity's window
lets you see a world
you didn't dream was there,
but if you dreamt it,
then it would not be
the window of opportunity.

A LESSON IN INFINITY

It wasn't the length of infinity
that caught my attention today
but rather the depth of numbers
which led me to think this way.

For God we know is infinite
in His own special style
but human beings are infinite too
and if this statement then is true,
there's a richness in people
of wonders unsought
by those who believe that they know
how self-sufficient their living is
but never attempt to grow.

DINOSAUR

How did the dinosaur
find his way across the world
into Wyoming's flats?
Was he created here
or did he migrate from afar?
I cannot quite see how his trail
crossed the vast expanse of earth
nor see him swamp born either
and yet one or the other
was his ancestry.

THE OLD HOUSE

I am a house, not young in years.
There are among you those who say
that house must have a tale to tell
and, oh, I do, for I was damned
before the first ones came to live
and so when shutters bang the wall
and shades flip up or doors fly shut,
they do not know the aggravating force
which causes such destruction here.

I am a house, condemned by her who died
by her own hand when first she learned
how traitorous her lover had been.
I am a house, grown old and closed
decay of years and loneliness destroyed me
for never was I what I meant to be
a home for her who found herself left out,
the jilted bride.

MEMORY IS STRANGE

THE SPACES IN MY MEMORY
WHAT DO THEY MEAN TO ME?
WHY CAN I THINK OF ONE SO WELL
AND FORGET TWO OR THREE?

WHAT IS IT THAT WE STORE SO DEEP
FOR GLIB RECALL SOME FUTURE DAY
AND PASS BY OTHERS SO WELL KNOWN?
I REALLY CANNOT SAY.

STILL WATERS

Still waters
quiet spots
we search for peace
where it is not.

Still waters
tortured soul
heal the hurts
make us whole.

HIS GLOBE

The picture was a globe, a jagged line divided it.
I looked and saw his world:
Along one side were home and Mom,
the pictures here were love and harmony,
and then upon the other side
were dope and drink and guns and crime.
I held it in my shaking hands.
The boy who had prepared it was
a lad whose background was confused
and yet as I perused its form
I knew that what he could not say
he had poured out in this crude art
and we were friends at last.

THE TEACHER'S REWARD

"I'm not an intellectual," I said
and yet I'm not without some learning true.
My years have nearly all been spent
with books and thoughts and searches too.
Those boys and girls whose minds I reached
have sought out goals I could not gain
but what they have achieved raised me
to heights where only adding other minds
could take me.

AMERICANS

Americans! We are a lot
of people strange from here and there.
We fume, we swear, we fuss
that change we seek cannot take place,
and then we set about to do it.
When it is done, you know, we brag
about that very turn
we once insisted not one soul could make.

NOVEMBER 10, 1989

Today the Berlin Wall came down,
that fearful wall across the town
which kept the East and West apart
What will it mean in thirty years:
another war or just new peace
across the European front?
And Checkpoint Charlie's trappings,
will they be scrapped or kept to help
remind mankind of human cruelty?
I wish I knew.

CHECKPOINT CHARLIE

Today I heard the phrase
called "Checkpoint Charlie"
but it was not Berlin they named
but some strange sounding name
the center of another war
in the far off Persian Gulf.

We never learn.

CAN YOU EXPLAIN

What put man upright on his legs
and turned him to the stars?
Oh, certainly it was not the same
as that which set up wars.

WORDS

Words!
We need them!
Could we survive
in our world?
What did man do
before words
What was he then?

ELDERHOSTLERS

Friendships are warm
Bedrooms are cool
Teachers are fun
We learn as a rule
We're called Elderhostlers
Or elderly hustlers
But the kids would be rushing
if they kept up with us
Wouldn't they?

SWEEPSTAKES

I dreamt I won the million
the contest said I could
and wondered what I'd use it for:
a house: I have a house.
a car: I like my car.
to educate myself: I have an education.
retirement: I am retired.
a trip somewhere I'd love to go:
my body says its time to stay
within the area where I dwell.
So why receive the million?
The rules state I could get some cash
each year for thirty more
And that's a laugh for sure.
I've reached my zenith
I'm on the downward cycle.
I don't have thirty years,
but I shall try to win it just the same.

FREEDOM

Liberty!
Freedom!
Just words?
The spirit can be free
although the body has
no liberty.

OUR MEAGER LANGUAGE

English is meager
in words of love,
and so we find
we have no meaning
for this word.
For what is LOVE?
The lust for another body,
the protection we give a child,
the feeling of home and land,
the search for God?
What is love?
all of these and more.
Our single word must be
encompassing for them all.

ALIENS

Must our country
continue
to accept all
who think us weak
yet want to share
our freedom?
Must our country accept,
or destroy them.

THIS GENERATION

Why do we race our lives away
and bind ourself with tasks?
Can man no longer take himself
at some face value and accept
his strengths, his limitations?

We constantly accept a load
of chores or titles for a group
and count our worth by jobs we've done.
The man who does his work and then
retires at home to read and think,
is queer somehow. He does not join
in that mad race which each small town
considers it must have to justify
the cash it spends, the loans it makes.

The doctrine of success
which says that one can be
whatever it is he wishes
does not say he can be happy there.
But one who finds that life
is full of joy must live it constantly
and while he may become a happy soul,
though others count him rich
he may not be.

A CHILD IN THE PARK

The pixie girl who danced
along the path ahead
in time to some sweet song
within her mind
stopped suddenly entranced.
The long straight line of geese
advanced across the lake
then all at once they veered
and spread across the sky
above her upturned head.

She watched till they were gone,
then walked in deepest thought
without another word of song
upon her quiet lips.

SHOCK

That moment of suspense
between the hurt and the cry
can be so brief
we do not see the space
and yet it's there.

FEATHERED THUNDERBIRDS

I never saw them there before
a flock of snow white gulls,
gray-tipped, upon the lake.
They swirled and zoomed
first high then low
upon the waves,
dive bombed to catch
a prey, then race
against the sky;
white angels there maneuvering about
just visitors from somewhere else
upon this lake of ours.

SPRING SIGN

The cedar waxwings came today,
they swirled across my view
into the juniper next door.
Alas! The drought last year left
no berries hanging on its limbs.
Those birds rose up in great alarm,
they gathered in a row upon the wires,
conferred, returned to check again,
then fled the scene,
a hungry, disappointed flock.

SAFETY PIN

Today I found a safety pin
and suddenly I thought
my dear, our lives are turned around
for what has velcro brought.

MEMORY

Some things
in the shadows of life
do not have to be
remembered.
They remember themselves.

AN IRISHER

The Irish, so they say,
talk their art away.
This I know is true,
for I'm a talker too.

TRIVIA

WRITING TRIVIA
THAT'S WHAT I DO
RANDOM THOUGHTS THAT RISE
IN ME AND YOU.
AND SO MY VERSES TOUCH YOU
DAY BY DAY
FOR THIS IS WHAT YOU THOUGHT OF TOO.

MY THEOREM

We know one law
and one alone
and have since time began,
that everything will change
and that includes
both Earth and Man.

LONELINESS

When no one is around
to see or to hear
your troubles seem greater
your joys disappear.

HIM OR HER — OF GOD?

Him or Her — of God?
The sexuality
concerns me? Yes.
For God made man
in His own image.
The ancients made man God
but both acclaimed to woman another place in life.
Her tasks were not the same.
Him or Her — of God!
What woman who knows
her worth would seek to be
a female God — or serve one.

A SAD SONG

I helped him raise our family
encouraged him at work
I nursed him back to health
and kept expenses within bounds
but never till the day he died
said he, "I love you!"

MY LIFE

I lived my life
I loved
I laughed
As through the world I went
I earned
a little cash
and what I earned I spent,
and here I come
to my old age
my heart still full of glee
for I have loved so much
there is no fretting time for me.

MODERN SONGS

What has become of moon,
and June and tune
in love songs today?
No longer are they full of bliss
the glory of a loving kiss
the signs that say "It's you I miss"
but rather, "Must you go away?"
"Why won't you stay?"
"Have you found another gal or guy?"
this is not love
it's just good-bye.

JOKE

Some places are so small
their breadth my hand can span
I know how it would feel
to be a tuna in a sardine can.

CAT SMELLS

My house still smelled of cat
my mother said,
although old Tiger had been gone
for many years.
And yet through all this time
I have not seen
a mouse around the place.
Can they smell cats?

DID YOU WONDER

Did you wonder?
Do you know?
If Aaron was the priest,
where did Moses learn
to read and write?
In Egypt?
Then why were the Commandments
not written in hieroglyphics.

CHANGE

No person's life is all her own,
if she be single and alone,
she longs for one to cherish her.
If she be married and a part
of life that quite surrounds her,
she longs for freedom from restraint.
No person's life is all her own,
Why do we think that change will satisfy?

WHAT'S YOUR EXCUSE?

Her house is unkempt.
Her dishes unwashed
no order in closet or drawer.
Her clothes disarranged
her hair is uncombed
and she is a mess
you would say.
But let her alone
don't hurry her so
a poem is brewing
and that's how I know
when her soul is so full of verse
her home is a windstorm — or worse.

Louise Flynn Underhill

Born in Du Quoin, Illinois, educated in Illinois and Kentucky, plus graduate courses in other states.

Published poetry since 1930. Teacher of English and journalism. Author of many articles, several treatises on education, and, since 1976, compiler of two cookbooks and publisher of eight books of her personal poetry.

Distinguished alumna award from Georgetown College (Ky), 1980. Listed in *Who's Who of American Women*. Honorary member of the International Guild of Women Writers. Active in clubs, fraternal orders, church, and politics.

Photograph of Louise F. Underhill by Olan Mills Co. 1990.

Other works:

Handbook for Beginning Sponsors of School Newspapers, by Dr. Joe Milner and Louise Flynn 1965

Yesterday's Minds or Tomorrow's, Creative Handbook for School District #1 Cheyenne, compiled and edited 1965

Active Dames Kookbook, co-edited with Mary Read Rodgers for Alpha Delta Kappa Sorority 1968

History of Carey Junior High School, compiled 1971

Red Hollyhocks 1976

The Moth 1977

Captain Jason and other Poems 1980

Mostly For Men, (cookbook) ed. 1979

Wyoming Moods 1980

My Exploding World 1983

Winds of My Mind 1986

Vapor Trails 1989.

Design by
James M. Beasley.

Printed by
Pioneer Printing and Stationery Co.
Cheyenne, Wyoming